A SHORT HANDBOOK AND STYLE SHEET

Thomas Pinney
Pomona College

HARCOURT BRACE JOVANOVICH, PUBLISHERS

San Diego   New York   Chicago   Austin
London   Sydney   Toronto

To Anne, Jane, and Sarah

ISBN: 0-15-580925-3

Library of Congress Catalog Card Number: 76-51133

Printed in the United States of America

ACKNOWLEDGMENTS

The author wishes to thank the following for permission to reprint copyrighted material:

Harcourt Brace Jovanovich, Inc., publishers, **Martin Secker & Warburg,** publishers, and **Mrs. Sonia Brownell Orwell,** copyright holder, for an excerpt from George Orwell, "Politics and the English Language," in *Shooting an Elephant and Other Essays* by George Orwell; and **Oxford University Press** for an excerpt from William Butler Yeats, *Letters on Poetry from W. B. Yeats to Dorothy Wellesley;* reprinted by permission of the Oxford University Press.

"Are you beginning to dislike slang, then?" said Rosamond, with mild gravity.

"Only the wrong sort. All choice of words is slang. It marks a class."

"There is correct English: that is not slang."

"I beg your pardon: correct English is the slang of prigs who write history and essays. And the strongest slang of all is the slang of poets."

—George Eliot, *Middlemarch*

There are nine and sixty ways of constructing tribal lays,
And-every-single-one-of-them-is-right!

—Rudyard Kipling, "In the Neolithic Age"

The correction of prose, because it has no fixed laws, is endless.

—William Butler Yeats, *Letters on Poetry from W. B. Yeats to Dorothy Wellesley*

Contents

A SHORT HANDBOOK

The Standard of Good Style   2
Diction   2
   Euphemisms   4
   Clichés   4
   Incoherent Figurative Language   5
   Unidiomatic Diction   6
   Jargon   7
Sentences   10
   Vagueness   11
   Inappropriate Use of the Passive Voice   12
   Wordiness   13
   Problems of Sentence Order and Variety   16
   Defective Subordination   17
Paragraphs   18
Some Particular Points of Grammar and
      Sentence Construction   19

Agreement   19
Reference   22
Misplaced Modifier   24
Dangling Element   24
Tense   26
Parallelism   26
Incongruity   27
Punctuation   31
Comma   32
Semicolon   34
Colon   37
Dash   37
Apostrophe and Quotation Marks   38
Punctuation for Emphasis   39
Mechanics: Spelling, Word Division, Capitalization   39
Spelling   39
Word Division   40
Capitalization   40

A SHORT STYLE SHEET

Format   41
Quotations   42
Acknowledgments and Footnotes   45
Parenthetical Notes   53
Bibliography   55
Miscellaneous Conventions   56
The Use of Italics or Underlining   56
Titles   56
Numbers   57
Abbreviations   58
Advice to the Writer (*inside back cover*)
A Marking Code (*back cover*)

A SHORT HANDBOOK

This short handbook is not a comprehensive list of rules. It is a summary guide to effective writing and to essential questions of format and editorial style. By identifying bad practices and by suggesting some better ones, it presents the choices that a writer must think about in order to get down what he wants to say in the way he wants to say it. Such choices have first to be made deliberately, by thinking about the alternatives; with practice, they can be made almost with the assurance of second nature. This book tries to help by describing a civilized ideal of prose and by pointing out some common pitfalls.

It perhaps need not be added that one learns to write only by writing and that one must have something to say as well as a method for saying it. But even much practice and a full mind will not automatically produce good writing; it is necessary to think about how you want to write, the means available, and the things to be avoided.

The Standard of Good Style

> No style is good that is not fit to be spoken or
> read aloud with effect.
>
> —William Hazlitt

Written composition differs from speech because we expect it to be logically and grammatically complete; its language should be thoughtfully chosen, and its constructions carefully fitted together. *But you should never write anything that you cannot at least imagine yourself saying.* If you deviate from this standard, then know why you do so. Good writing is not identical with unnaturally formal writing.

Diction

> I would never use a long word where a short
> one would answer the purpose. I know there
> are professors in this country who "ligate"
> arteries. Other surgeons only tie them, and it
> stops the bleeding just as well.
>
> —Oliver Wendell Holmes

ⅾ Diction means the choice of words from the entire range provided by the language, the huge stock of words recorded in the dictionary. Its ideal principle is *le mot juste*—the right word in the right place—but the fitness of a word by itself can never be determined. No word is a bad word, although words may express bad things; one can distinguish only between uses, misuses, and abuses of words.

Typically, books of advice to writers urge the virtues of correctness, accuracy, and clarity in the matter of diction, but again these virtues are functions of actual use, not qualities ⱳⱳ inherent in particular words. Lexical correctness—whether a word *means* what the writer thinks it does or not—can of course be readily determined by reference to a dictionary. But a word can be accurate and clear only according to how it is used. It is important to see this point, because otherwise one may fall into the mistake of attributing to words the faults that belong to a writer's use of them.

With that general reservation out of the way, one comprehensive principle of style will help to resolve many questions as to the choice of words: prefer simple or everyday language to fancy language. Write *begin,* not *commence; before,* not *prior to; use,* not *utilize; end,* not *termination,* and let the rest of your language be in keeping with those simple words. Nothing can conceal poverty of thought—especially from the writer himself—more effectively than fancy language. If you really have something to say, perspicuous language allows it to be seen. One need not make a fetish of one-syllable words, or reject all latinate phrases—like the "perspicuous language" that I just used—in order to achieve plainness. But for most of us it requires constant attentiveness to write in a way that would be pleasant to hear rather than impressive to look at.

The question seems to be social as much as or more than technical, for your choice of language is largely determined by your attitude toward your reader, and is therefore a question of manners. Who do you want to sound like? Who are you trying to impress? And can you run the risk of being clear and agreeable instead of hiding behind a mask of opaque language?

The anxiety felt by many writers in using simple language shows up in the trick of putting what they feel to be unsuitable words or phrases in the pillory of quotation marks:

I have had long experience at counseling and "selling ideas" to others.

By this means, writers dissociate themselves from what they have written. But if you think that a word or phrase is wrong, don't use it; if it is the phrase that you want, use it without apology. And never apologize for simple and idiomatic language.

Some particular faults of diction to be recognized and avoided follow.

Euphemisms

> When one is polite in German, one lies.
>
> —Goethe

Goethe's epigram applies to English too. Euphemisms—the word comes from the Greek for "sounding good"—are polite or pretentious forms usually intended to conceal something unpleasant or embarrassing and are thus ways of telling lies: *passed away* for *died; senior citizen* for *old person; exceptional* for *handicapped; disadvantaged* for *poor*.

There are times—many times—when euphemisms are appropriate and desirable: social life would be impossible without them, for a spade cannot always be called a spade. But using euphemisms should be an act of choice and not of ignorance or insensibility. Our times are rich in euphemisms, and to be able to avoid a helpless dependence on them is a real test of style.

Clichés

> Originality does not consist in saying what no one has ever said before, but in saying exactly what you think yourself.
>
> —Leslie Stephen

Words and phrases that have been overused and that appear automatically in certain situations are called "clichés"; the French word means the same thing as the English "stereotypes," and both words contain the idea of something fixed and unvarying. Clichés are almost always metaphorical, but through overwork the metaphor has died; that is, it is no longer perceived as a figurative expression but as a mere neutral form of words. For example:

to the bitter end	silver lining
last but not least	take by storm
nip in the bud	in the final analysis
leave no stone unturned	rugged individualist
seamy side of life	tried and true

The real objection to clichés, apart from their stale familiarity and their predictability, is that they offer prefabricated phrasing that may be used without effort on your part. They are thus used at the expense of both individuality and precision, since you can't say just what you mean in the mechanical response of a cliché.

Such, at any rate, is the extreme form of the argument. But there are, inevitably, many occasions when the convenient formula of a cliché is the readiest, most efficient way of expressing your thought. In that case, go ahead. It would be hard, for example, to do without phrases like "I smell a rat," or the myriad small, fixed phrases that enable us to talk and write fluently. I have used many in this brief discussion (for example, "brief discussion"), just as I talked about "calling a spade a spade" in the section on euphemisms. What this reflection suggests is that clichés, like words themselves, are not · inherently objectionable; the test is *appropriateness.* If, for example, you wish to say that a girl is waiting patiently, is it appropriate to use the cliché that "she sat like patience on a monument" (Shakespeare, but still a cliché)? Or is the cliché an impertinence? Perhaps she's standing? or quietly moving about? If, in enumerating a sequence, you come to the end by saying "last but not least," is that the fact? or just a reflex phrase, without point?

One final point about clichés: if you use one, be sure that you get it right. If you write "take it for granite" instead of *granted,* or "put him on his metal" for *mettle,* you commit the kind of error known as a schoolboy boner and will be laughed at.

Incoherent Figurative Language

Writers who do not attend to the figurative element in their language will regularly produce grotesque and inadvertently comic mixtures:

> Twain shows freedom to be a staggering and demoralizing burden on the individual that lends insight into problems that seem unsolvable.

The combination of physical ("staggering") and spiritual ("demoralizing") effects produced by a metaphorical "burden" that is somehow capable of "lending insight" is a strange mishmash. No one would write in that way purposely, and yet people do write in that way. The only acceptable explanation is that such writers are paying no attention to the images and suggestions created by the language that they use. They are not necessarily writing carelessly or indifferently; unfortunately, very hard and well meant effort may all too easily produce such results. But they do not see what they are doing. Consider another example:

> This background, then, was fed and fanned by Romantic ideals, and the story of Turner's development thus blossoms into a driving force.

Can you draw a picture of a Romantic Ideal feeding and fanning a background? or of a driving force that blossomed out of a development? Even James Thurber might have found these strange conjunctions beyond his powers of comic drawing. Dead metaphors, invisible to the writer, have been galvanized into a spasmodic moment of comic life by this unthinking juxtaposition. If the writer had made any attempt to see the figure he was creating, he would have recognized its monstrosity at once.

Unidiomatic Diction

idiom By "idiom" is meant not some deplorable lapse but simply those patterns of the language that are not matters of rule but of habit and general practice. To speak idiomatically is to speak well.

Unidiomatic language is created when a writer is being formal and falls into a style never heard on land or sea:

> He aided her in becoming acquainted with the main aspects involved in such a career.

> I am effective in facilitating students to establish goals and set priorities.

The writers of such sentences are evidently frightened to write as they think or speak, and so produce this awkward, unidiomatic style. A more conversational style is better; the fact that it may take more words is not a fault, if the longer version is more distinct and idiomatic:

> He helped her to learn about the skills required, the problems that might arise, and the opportunities available in such a career.

In the second example, "facilitating" is not absolutely wrong, but surely we facilitate things rather than people? The choice is unidiomatic: we don't hear it. One would say something like this:

> I am good at helping students to establish goals and set priorities.

The cure for unidiomatic diction is to trust your sense of what you actually hear. Don't write what you have never heard said, or cannot imagine being said by anyone worth listening to.

Jargon

> That must be fine, for I don't understand a word.
> —Molière, *The Physician in Spite of Himself*

The word "jargon" comes from the old French and originally meant the twittering of birds or an unintelligible chattering. It has since come to mean two different but related things: the technical language of a craft or profession, or any language that seems obscure, pretentious, and unattractive. Drawing the line between jargon in the first sense—legitimate technical language—and jargon in the second is not always easy. There is, however, reasonable agreement as to the character of jargon in the second, bad sense. Here are some unmistakable symptoms of the disease. If several of them occur together, the diagnosis of jargon is almost certain.

1. The passive voice drives out the active.

2. Verbs disappear, except for forms of *to be*.

3. All simple terms are expanded:
   > *is indicative of* for *indicates*
   > *is supportive of* for *supports*
   > *in the event that* for *if*
   > *in view of the fact that* for *since*

4. Long strings of prepositional phrases, without emphasis and seemingly without end, proliferate:
   > The problem *of* order, and thus *of* the nature *of* the integration *of* stable systems *of* social integration . . .

5. Sentences are inflated by abstract phrases, dead metaphors, empty terms:
   > activity ("major shower activity")
   > facet
   > field ("one facet of this field")
   > factor
   > in terms of ("the factors in terms of expenditure are cost-prohibitive")
   > of this nature ("the sky is of a blue nature")
   > situation
   > type ("a third-down type of situation")

   By these means, simple propositions may be entirely transformed:
   > The situation in terms of weather is indicative of major shower activity.
   > *Translation:* It looks like rain.

6. Modish terms abound. Here are some current favorites:
   > charismatic
   > dialogue
   > dichotomy
   > educator
   > implement (verb)
   > interpersonal
   > life style (or lifestyle)
   > massive ("after World War II Europe was in a massive state of disarray")

orient (verb)
perspective
polarized ("an exchange of their respective polarized
sexual elements")
posture
relate
societal
thrust ("the thrust of his posture was toward détente")
viable

7. New coinages flourish

 a. with *ize* and *wise:*
 Theaterwise, the impact of *Gone with the Wind* has
 been totally maximized.

 The superintendent is going to have to reprioritize
 his thinking budgetwise.

 b. by converting one part of speech into another:
 He has authored six books.

 They are real love persons in a now situation.

This convertibility of nouns to verbs, verbs to nouns, adjectives to adverbs, and so on, is natural to English, but
the very ease of such transformation is a reason to be cau-
tious about it.

8. Noun-noun constructions multiply:

 annual cohort size adjustment mechanism
 diversified creativity interest areas
 national origin minority school children
 Orange County Council Environment Employment
 Economy Development (There really is such a
 thing—but what can it be?)

9. Unrelieved abstraction prevails and nobody does anything: commodities are utilized, parameters are considered, factors are hypothesized, and so on. The world of
 people and things is vaporized.

10. Resounding nonsense abounds:
 Throughout the book, freedom is shown as a state of
 being that allows for internal and external insight, a con-
 straint upon social mechanisms and interaction, and as
 a counterpoint to intellectual confinement.

The conventions of technical writing dictate many of the elements of jargon, for example, abstraction, impersonality, hard words, the passive voice (although that requirement is changing: see p. 13). However, a writer still has an important range of choice between more or less wordiness, more or less stereotyped language, more or less use of dull noun and prepositional phrases, more or less deviation from the standard of educated conversational discourse. The key lies in the writer's intention. If he wishes to show courtesy to his reader, he can. He should also want his performance to give some pleasure to himself through its style.

Sentences

F The elementary fault in the construction of sentences is in not recognizing an incomplete form:

> To tell the truth.
>
> Since he isn't here.
>
> Concerning the "Star Spangled Banner," of which the lyrics are not coherent and peaceful.

These are sentence parts, not whole sentences, and to write thus is illiterate. By way of exception, some sentence fragments are allowable for special effect, especially if you wish to imitate the rhythms of speech:

> I wouldn't dream of it. Not much.
>
> Just my luck. Nobody home. Nobody.

Advertising writers are particularly fond of this trick—a reason, I think, to avoid it:

> Get into a Fury today. At your Chrysler-Plymouth dealer.

After the rule of completeness, the general principle in writing sentences is to say something distinct. Some of the main obstacles in the way of this simple object follow.

Vagueness

It is easy to write sentences that are complete in every gram-   vague
matical sense but that say nothing, or nothing much, because
they do not specify anything.

> One of the things that I liked about her was her really nice per-
> sonality.

> Things in the Middle East gave Kissinger some trouble.

> Las Vegas boasts many achievements that make it an ideal
> city.

Some analyzable sources of vagueness, apart from sheer
mental vacuity, are these:

Empty Generalizations

Empty generalizations are often encountered at the beginning of paragraphs, where they provide the writer a means to
get started:

> The system has some very interesting aspects.

Try instead to name the ideas that you mean:

> The system is an interesting attempt to combine freedom with
> order.

Overemphasized and Inflated Phrases

> *Throughout much* of the *earlier part* of this century there was a
> great deal of discussion about the desirability and use of the
> federal tax mechanism on corporate structure.

The words italicized seem to stand for something distinct, but
don't really.

> *In the earlier part* of this century . . .

is all that can be safely deduced from the phrase.

Indistinct Relationships

The vaguely inclusive use of the connective word "with" is the most common instance of this fault:

> Randy had a lot of trouble in Tijuana, *with* many things not what he expected at all.

Try to name what is meant:

> Randy had a lot of trouble in Tijuana: he didn't expect to be searched at the bridge, or to have his hubcaps stolen, or, worst of all, to come down with the *turista.*

> Architecture, art, and literature were all greatly affected by the Gothic Revival, *with* some very important medievally oriented works of literature left as a legacy.

In the second example, it is almost impossible to say what the "with" phrase can mean; one possibility is:

> Although architecture and art were greatly affected by the Gothic Revival, its deepest influence was on literature.

But the relational force of the "with" is so feeble that one can only guess.

Inappropriate Use of the Passive Voice

passive   The difference between what grammarians call the active and the passive voices is easily illustrated:

> **Active:**   Joe ate the pie.
> **Passive:**   The pie was eaten.

In the active voice the subject is doing something; in the passive, the subject is being acted upon. Therefore, whenever the emphasis is on the thing done rather than the doer, the passive voice has its proper use; it is a way of shifting the focus from sentence to sentence. The passive voice is not "wrong": it is an integral part of the English language. But ordinarily we take the active voice as standard in idiomatic speech: in conversation one would always say "I went to the movies" or "I spent the summer at the beach" rather than "the movies were attended" or "the summer was spent at the beach." In the world of everyday things to which such sentences belong, one naturally expects to be told who is doing the things described. The passive is not what one would hear, and its use would be just as inappropriate in writing about such things as in speaking about them.

The passive voice used to be required as an ironclad convention in scientific reporting:

> ***Not:*** I then added six cubic centimeters.
> ***But:*** Six cubic centimeters were then added.

The emphasis on the explanation of processes in scientific writing means that such writing will always give a special preference to the passive voice. But even in scientific writing the convention is changing in favor of a more natural, less rigidly impersonal manner. The editors of *Science,* for example, instruct their writers to "choose the active voice more often than you choose the passive, for the passive voice usually requires more words and often obscures the agent of the action." One must repeat that the passive is a legitimate and necessary form, not to be treated as taboo; the advice to prefer the active rests entirely on the fact that it is generally the more idiomatic form, not that it is in some abstract way the better form.

Wordiness

> As a general rule, run your pen through every other word you have written; you have no idea what vigor it will give to your style.
>
> —Sydney Smith

Wordiness, like so many other faults of writing, is not a qual- w ity that can be simply measured. It is obviously not the fact that the fewer the words the better the writing—otherwise the model of style would be a telegram. The real ground of wordiness is not length but inefficiency. Sentences loaded with words and phrases that do not have any genuine expressive function but are merely fillers or flourishes are properly said to be wordy. Here are some types of wordiness:

Small-change Constructions

Phrases and words such as "due to the fact that," "basically," "in terms of," "in regard to," and the like are the ready means by which we maintain fluency in speech. They can be used to spin out talk indefinitely. They don't say much, but are a sort of small change that one can carry about for spending on any unimportant occasion. Whenever you catch yourself using one of these links or qualifiers, think twice. Almost certainly you can do without it, or put your thought in terms both more specific and more appropriate.

> In regard to this consideration we are preparing a revised statement.

Simply do without the suspect phrase:

> We are preparing a revised statement.

Be especially wary of factitious intensifiers such as "definitely," "obviously," "really," "very." Save them for when you mean them.

Redundancies and Repetitions

Avoid such mindless doublings and triplings of the same meaning as are exhibited in these examples:

> **Not:** The situation in our modern world of today
> **But:** The situation in our world
> **Or:** The situation in the modern world
>
> **Not:** Fundamentally, the most basic reason is cost.
> **But:** Cost is the basic reason.

When the same word or phrase appears in two or more successive sentences, try to get rid of the repetition by combining the sentences or by eliminating one or more of the repeated elements:

It is interesting to contrast the two *descriptions.* The first *description* is complete; the second *description* is not complete.

In this case, correct simply by dropping the repeated words:

It is interesting to contrast the two descriptions. The first is complete; the second is not.

See also *Primer Style,* p. 16.

Impertinences and Superfluities

Do not insult the reader with gratuitous information or irrelevant description:

Not: The celebrated tragic masterwork, *Hamlet,* by the greatest of English dramatists, William Shakespeare, expresses Elizabethan political values.

But: *Hamlet* expresses Elizabethan political values.

Impersonal Constructions

Impersonal constructions are those forms in which the ordinary personal subject is displaced by an expletive (that is, a filler word) or by a subject in the third person. In the sentence "There are three cats here," *there* is an expletive. In the sentence "The experimenter then applied the selected stimulus," *the experimenter* is an impersonal subject. While both expletives and impersonal subjects are proper and useful devices of language, trouble arises when they are habitually and monotonously employed:

The writer has observed that it is often the case that there are numerous forms of political reaction in times of economic depression.

The cure for such bloodless and wordy constructions is to get rid of the impersonality and the expletives:

> I have observed that times of economic depression often generate numerous forms of political reaction.

Impersonality is usually allied with the passive voice, often in the name of scientific objectivity:

> The classification of subjects' responses was then carried out by the researcher in accordance with the previously established procedures.

Many scientific journals, however, now encourage their contributors to relax from such austere impersonality and to write in a way that reveals the presence of a person at work:

> *Not:*   This reporter then inquired
> *But:*   I then asked
>
> *Not:*   It is felt that
> *But:*   I think

Compare the section on the use of the passive voice, p. 12.

The commonest of wordy forms are the impersonal phrases *there is, there are, it is,* often in conjunction with *which* and *that:*

> There are three factors *that* influenced this decision.

The sentence is not vicious in itself, but the style must not be overworked. Try instead:

> Three factors influenced this decision.

Problems of Sentence Order and Variety

pr *Primer Style*

The normal order of sentences in English is subject-verb-object. Variation from that order merely for the sake of variation is a poor rule. But one should try to avoid a succession of simple, monotonous declarative sentences in the fashion of grade school readers:

> This church embodies the Gothic spirit Pugin was trying to revive in England. It evokes the magnificence of God. It is designed to celebrate the glory of God. This church represents the theology of the Catholic faith. The church is built on the foundations of Christian architecture. The foundations are not architectural but religious.

See also *Redundancies and Repetitions,* p. 14.

Run-on Sentences   run-on

Run-on sentences exhibit primer style within the limits of a single sentence by simply accumulating coordinate phrases and clauses:

> Vivien Leigh was anxious to play Scarlett O'Hara, and she was glad to get the chance, but she did not know what a great success she would have, and she was not prepared for the tremendous fame it brought.

Defective Subordination

The form of a sentence should correspond to the logic of su what is being said.

Main Ideas Should Not Be Put in Subordinate Form

> He went to the races at Del Mar yesterday, thus losing all of his money.

The second part of the sentence should be made at least equal to the first:

> He went to the races at Del Mar yesterday and lost all of his money.

Or it should become the main statement:

> When he went to the races at Del Mar yesterday, he lost all of his money.

Unequal Things Should Not Be Made Equal in Form

> Fitzgerald attended prep school and entered Princeton in 1913.

Here a dependent or subsidiary idea is given equal footing with a main idea, and no explanation of their relation is provided. To correct, change the relation of parts:

> After attending prep school, Fitzgerald entered Princeton in 1913.

Sentences that confuse or invert the relationship between major and minor propositions or between cause and effect are very damaging to a reader's confidence in the writer.

Paragraphs

unity Paragraphs ought to have unity; that is, they should stick to a single idea or subject and omit all irrelevant matter. Relevance will depend not only on ordinary logic but on the point of view and the understanding that you bring to the subject; the organization of paragraphs is thus a crucial measure of the writer's control.

coh Paragraphs should also be coherent; that is, they should organize related material into an appropriate order, appropriateness again being determined by the writer's purpose. Connections of thought between paragraphs (and within *tr* them too) should be made clear by appropriate transitions: the reader should not be made to leap from one part to the next, nor to puzzle over how one point follows from another.

As a rule, don't write paragraphs of less than three sentences (unless you are writing something studiedly brief, like this handbook). Either develop the idea, make it a subordinate part of some other paragraph, or discard it. Abbreviated paragraphs—all too familiar from tabloid journalism, from television newscasting, and from the rhetoric of advertising—make the development of thought impossible and insult the intelligence of the reader, who is assumed to possess an attention span of a few seconds only.

Introductory paragraphs should really introduce what is to follow. An introduction is not just a statement of what you are going to do; it is, rather, an explanation of why you are doing what you are doing, or why the question you are asking is worth asking. Concluding paragraphs should really conclude. A conclusion is not a restatement of what you have just done, but a reflection on it, or a new turn, or an application of your point. In a short composition, especially, one should be very harsh in judging introductory and final paragraphs. If the opening or closing paragraph is merely a ceremonial statement, cut it out. In a long text—so long that the contents cannot be readily grasped as a unified discourse—an introductory prospectus and a closing retrospect may be valuable. Such things are almost always a waste of time in a short composition.

Some Particular Points of Grammar and Sentence Construction

Agreement

A Verb Must Agree with Its Subject in Number and Person

Everyone knows how to manage this:

number $\begin{cases}$ *Sally* never *fails* to choose the right answer.
Sally and *David* never *fail* to miss the point. $\end{cases}$

person $\begin{cases}$ *I know* little about it.
He knows it all. $\end{cases}$

At times, however, determining agreement between subject and verb isn't quite so simple. The most common sources of trouble in handling agreement involve:

Collective Nouns   Collective nouns are those words which name groups or organizations—the Detroit Tigers, the Republican party, the British government—that have an individual identity but that are composed of many individuals. Such subjects can be treated as either singular or plural depending on how they are thought of, but be consistent in your treatment. Avoid the inattentive wavering between singular and plural shown in these examples:

> The faculty *is* going to try to restore the F grade, but *they* have a surprise in store for them.

> Each year at this time CBS *announces their* choice of athlete of the year.

> We the people of Howard Johnson's are proud to be a part of *these* great United States as *she* approaches her 200th birthday.

Relative Clauses   Errors of agreement arise when the antecedent of a relative pronoun and the subject of the sentence have different numbers.

> He's one of those dogs who always (barks/bark) at strangers.

Who is dependent on *dogs* and is therefore plural; *bark* is correct. One must not let the pull of the singular subject confuse the relation.

> Apples are a kind of fruit which always (has/have) to be winter-chilled.

The *which* depends on the singular *kind,* not on the plural *apples; has* is correct.

Subject and Complement of Different Numbers   When the verb *to be* links a plural subject to a singular complement, or links a singular subject to a plural complement, the rule is to let what comes first decide the question of number:

> Hitchcock's best *work is* (not *are*) his early *movies.*

or:

> Hitchcock's early *movies are* (not *is*) his best *work.*

Foreign Words A number of foreign words naturalized in English retain their native singular and plural forms. *Data, criteria, phenomena,* are the most familiar instances: all of these have the Latin or Greek plural ending in *a.* The singular forms are *datum, criterion, phenomenon,* and unless you are writing for a very uncritical audience you should observe the difference carefully. Some cases are unsettled:

> Graffiti has reached the point of uncivilized acceptance.

Graffiti is an Italian plural (the singular is *graffito*), but it is evidently understood here as a collective noun with singular meaning. Perhaps that is how we will all eventually understand it.

*A Pronoun Must Agree with Its Antecedent
in Number, Gender, and Person*

The agreement of definite pronouns with antecedents presents no particular trouble:

> Although *Sherrill* is a wife and mother, *she* is also a working woman.

> *Terry* and *Chuck* have just bought a new *house* and a new *car;* *they* can't pay for either but *they* certainly enjoy *them* both.

Indefinite pronouns such as *everyone, none, somebody, each,* are more problematic. Strictly, they are singular; *none* equals *no one,* and *one* is incontrovertibly only one. But in use they are often felt to be plural, and so confusions are created:

> Everyone paid for his dinner.
> Everyone paid for their dinner.
> Everyone paid for his dinners.
> Everyone paid for their dinners.

None of these feels exactly right, although the first example is technically correct. When you face such choices, consider rephrasing the sentence:

Each one paid for his dinner.

The strict adherence to the rule of making indefinite pronouns singular runs into the sexist question in language. Suppose, in the group named "each one," that there are five women and one man? "His/her" is now frequently seen as a way out:

Each one paid for his/her dinner.

But this solution is awkward at best, and it is too soon to know whether it will become standard.

ᴘ *Reference*

*A Definite Pronoun Must Refer Clearly
to a Specific Antecedent*

In Selznick's *Gone with the Wind,* he had the problem of controlling two difficult stars.

He has no proper antecedent, since the subject to which it refers is *Gone with the Wind,* not Selznick. *Selznick's* is a possessive adjective in the sentence; taking such adjectives for antecedents is a common source of mistakes in pronoun reference. The correction lies in getting the right subject into the sentence:

In *Gone with the Wind,* Selznick had the problem of controlling two difficult stars.

Avoid incongruous references:

Not: A director must be tough, but *it* mustn't be obvious to the actors.

But: A director must be tough, but not in a way that's obvious to the actors.

Not: His mother had rich relatives, and *it* gave him a taste for the life of the wealthy.

But: His mother had rich relatives, who gave him a taste for the life of the wealthy.

Avoid sentences in which the pronoun has more than one possible antecedent:

> The waiter took the dishes from the tables in order to clean *them.*

What did he clean?

> Senator Goldwater proposed an amendment to the administration's tax bill, *which* was strongly supported by the John Birch Society.

That may mean either:

> Senator Goldwater's proposed amendment to the administration's tax bill was strongly supported by the John Birch Society.

or:

> Senator Goldwater proposed an amendment to the administration's tax bill, a bill that was strongly supported by the John Birch Society.

The pronouns *this, that, which,* are regularly used to refer to general rather than to specific antecedents, but their use in that way is a common cause of looseness and vagueness (as it would be if *this* replaced *their use in that way* in the sentence you just read). The approximate, all-purpose uses of *this* to indicate any antecedent whatever—large, small, or even nonexistent—is a peculiarly common fault in writing.

> He is into transcendental meditation and macrobiotics. *This* is not going to get him anywhere with Sally.

> Charles is bright but not conceited, confident but not aggressive; *this* is why he is so successful.

Watch what you write to see whether you are using "this" in a succession of sentences:

This ruling had a particularly damaging effect on *this* country's wine trade. *This* meant that *this* industry had to make adjustments to meet *this* new standard. *This* was bound to be difficult.

mp *Misplaced Modifier*

Word order is the most important grammatical device in English, and no native speaker has any real trouble with it if he pays attention. The general rule is that modifying terms should be placed close to the terms that they modify:

Not: As I see it, the problem of *Hamlet* has *only* been coherently solved by Jones's psychoanalytic interpretation.

But: As I see it, the problem of *Hamlet* has been coherently solved *only* by Jones's psychoanalytic interpretation.

Not: Last week a delightful new children's play opened at our community theater called *The Treasure.*

But: Last week a delightful new children's play called *The Treasure* opened at our community theater.

Sometimes ambiguities exist even when the modifier is placed close to the term it modifies:

Mill and Arnold resumed their discussion automatically ignoring the visitor.

In this case the ambiguity can be resolved by placing a comma either before or after "automatically" to show what word is being modified.

da *Dangling Element*

A modifying phrase that has no proper subject to connect with in the main clause is said to "dangle" because it has nothing to stand on. More often than not, a dangling element seems to connect with a subject to which it does not belong and thus becomes a source of unintended comic effect:

Queen Victoria brought the waltz back into fashion, *after being considered indecent by Lord Byron and his generation.*

The only subject to which, grammatically, the modifying phrase can be attached is *Queen Victoria.* The correction lies in getting the proper term—*waltz*—into the sentence as its subject, or in making the dangling element a clause with its own subject, thus:

> *Either:*   The waltz, after being considered indecent by Lord Byron and his generation, was brought back into fashion by Queen Victoria.
>
> *Or:*   Queen Victoria brought the waltz back into fashion after it had been considered indecent by Lord Byron and his generation.

Nobody would misunderstand the sentence in its original form, but why look foolish? It is pleasing to think that Queen Victoria might have scandalized Lord Byron, but we know better.

In the next example the use of the passive voice presents an inappropriate subject so that the introductory phrase dangles:

> To maintain health, exercise must be taken.

Put the sentence in active form and you solve the problem:

> To maintain health, you must exercise.

So-called elliptical phrases also invite dangling constructions:

> Called the Jazz Age, or the Roaring 20s, America in the 1920s was an exciting place.

Correct by getting the right subject into the sentence:

> Called the Jazz Age, or the Roaring 20s, the decade of the 1920s was an exciting time in America.

Tense

Do not shift from one tense to another without a reason:

> Patton was intensely eager to break through the German lines and began the attack long before it had been scheduled. Eisenhower finally has to order him to halt.

The shift to the present tense in the second sentence makes no evident sense.

In writing anything historical, including reports of scientific experiments, one generally uses the past tense, for the activity being described has been completed. Note, however, that in writing about works of art the convention is to use the present tense, since works of fiction, paintings, or pieces of music are present in each new reading, viewing, or hearing:

> Napoleon *died* at St. Helena on 5 May 1821.
> **But:** The soldiers *bear* Hamlet to the ramparts.
> **Or:** The Mona Lisa still *smiles* her enigmatic smile.

pl *Parallelism*

Sentence elements that are parallel in thought and function must be parallel in form. Some common varieties of error follow.

Inconsistency in Series

> What Randall wants in a mare are beauty, health, breeding, and she must be docile.

The failure of the last term to match the rest is especially obvious in a compact series.

Imperfect Coordinate Structures

Sentences constructed with *and that* or *and which* need a preceding *that* or *which*:

Jane thought *Gone with the Wind* was the best movie and that Clark Gable made it so.

Correct by beginning "Jane thought *that* . . ."

The correlative terms *not only* . . . *but* introduce parallel phrases. It is also necessary to get the *not only* in the right place (see *Misplaced Modifier,* p. 24):

> ***Not:***   Not only was *Gone with the Wind* a financial success, but it also ranked high as an artistic effort.
>
> ***But:***   *Gone with the Wind* was not only a financial but an artistic success.

Shifts of Subject

> For years the records of the bank were kept in ledgers, while now electronic punch cards are employed.

The sentence begins with "records" as the subject but ends with "cards." Keeping the subject parallel sets the sentence straight:

> For years the *records* of the bank were kept in ledgers; now *they* are kept on electronic punch cards.

Incongruity

Faults of logic—confusions of categories, non sequiturs, contradictions, and so on—are not the province of the grammarian or the stylist, although obviously they will be among the main objects of attention for a critical reader. But in some cases, the link between grammar and logic is so close that the two can hardly be separated; such cases are here treated under the term incongruity,* a general term to indicate all of those many discords of grammar and logic that are not specifically covered by other categories. The term is not very pre-

---

* I owe the term to Robert Waddell, *Grammar and Style* (New York, 1951), chap. 15.

cise, since it must refer to many different things, but it is convenient. Some common forms of error follow.

Incongruity Between Subject and Complement

The most common incongruity arises in statements using some form of the verb *to be,* implying an equation between subject and complement:

> An *example* of the taste for nostalgia is *when* people flock to see movies about the fifties.

An *example* is not a *when;* the linking of the two terms by *is* constitutes simple grammatical and logical incongruity.

> The *reason* for the American love of violence is *on the basis of* the American past.

Reason and *on the basis of* don't match, although the linking verb *is* implies that they do: the one is a noun, the other an adverbial phrase. The structure is incongruously mixed.

A related error comes from using appositives that don't fit:

> I hope to get into medical school, a type of career that really attracts me.

> There is a mob violence scene, a recurrent theme in later Twain works.

A *school* is not a *career;* a *scene* is not a *theme.*

Besides that indicated by forms of the verb *to be,* other relations between a subject and a complement may be misstated:

> His intolerance of defeat even shows up in Notre Dame's losses.

His *intolerance* has no way of getting into *Notre Dame's losses,* so it can't *show up in* them. As a guess—and one can only guess at the meaning of so slovenly a sentence—one might try:

His intolerance of defeat is especially evident when Notre Dame loses.

Incongruous Figures and Phrases

Images and phrases that don't fit the sense of a statement are incongruous (see *Diction*, pp. 5–6):

> The meaning of *Robinson Crusoe* deals with the experience of solitude.
>
> The story of *Gone with the Wind* revolves around the Civil War.

Meanings don't *deal with:* one may deal with meanings, but they themselves simply are. And what does a story revolving around a war look like? Again, the verb is incongruous.

Illogical Comparisons

The terms of a comparison should match in form and logic, and both sides should be specified (faults of comparison may often be identified as faults of parallelism as well: see pp. 26–27):

> Sarah liked horses better because they were more fun.

The sentence exhibits incomplete comparisons—better than what? more fun than what? The model for such constructions is the so-called Ad Agency Comparative—"Freebies are bigger"—and although the usage is overwhelmingly established one can still call attention to its defects.

The commonest of incongruities through comparison is the comparison of things not equivalent:

> Anne thought that the meaning of *Jaws* was more profound than *The Towering Inferno*.

Here meaning is balanced not against meaning but against a title. Both grammar and logic require a comparison of like with like, as in this corrected sentence:

> Anne thought that the meaning of *Jaws* was more profound than that of *The Towering Inferno*.

Another sort of illogicality in comparison is the treatment of two classes as one:

> The director of *Gone with the Wind* was not trying to create thrills, unlike the other mercenary directors in Hollywood.

The *other* implies that all directors belong to the single class of mercenary directors, whereas the evident sense of the sentence is that there are two classes, mercenary and otherwise.

Illogical Qualifications

To qualify words which do not logically admit of qualification is incongruous. Presumably nobody would say that someone is "slightly dead" or a "little bit pregnant," but sentences like the following are common:

> The success of a picture like *Gone with the Wind* is *very* unique.
>
> He moves about in a social sphere which *partly* encompasses everyone.
>
> The character of the heroine is the *most* essential to the story.

Things are either unique or not, as they are either encompassed or not, essential or not.

Unmatched Numbers

Grammatical number should correspond to the sense of what is being said:

> A very large shark can easily bite their leg off.
>
> In the 1970s some new cars began to be built with an aluminum engine.

Many people seem to drift without bothering or even knowing how to steer their own course in life.

There are not enough legs and engines and courses to go around here (compare *Agreement,* p. 19).

Punctuation

> Punctuation, like usage, is an element of style, and the skillful writer can put much meaning into the placement of a comma.
>
> —"A Guide to Punctuation,"
> *Funk and Wagnalls*
> *Standard College Dictionary*

No brief handbook can attempt to cover all the details in the 𝕡 use of punctuation. Fortunately, there is a ready source of help. Every good desk dictionary contains a full, illustrated description of current conventions of punctuation.* When in doubt on some special question of punctuation, consult your dictionary.

Two general rules may be relied on: be consistent; and don't guess. If you haven't a clue, then it is better to leave out marks of punctuation rather than to sprinkle them indiscriminately over a page.

Apart from such rock bottom matters as beginning sentences with a capital letter and ending them with a period, the main rules of punctuation that *every* writer should know and apply with complete certainty follow.

---

* These are currently the most widely used dictionaries:

The American College Dictionary, revised ed., New York, Random House, 1969.

The American Heritage Dictionary of the English Language, Boston, Houghton Mifflin Company, 1969.

Funk and Wagnalls Standard College Dictionary, new ed., New York, Funk and Wagnalls, 1968.

Webster's New Collegiate Dictionary, Springfield, G. and C. Merriam Co., 1973.

Webster's New World Dictionary of the American Language, 2nd college ed., Cleveland and New York, Collins & World Publishing Co., 1974.

Comma

Use a Comma Between the Clauses of a Compound Sentence Joined by a Coordinating Conjunction

> The mariner shoots the albatross, *and* the ship is driven to a motionless sea.
>
> The Victorian woman's place was in the home, *but* not every woman liked the place.

The coordinating conjunctions are these:

and	so	but	or
for	yet	nor	

Exception | Between two short and simple main clauses the comma may be omitted:

> Jack was fat and Jill was thin.
>
> George collapsed but I kept going.

Do not confuse a compound sentence with a compound predicate:

> He worked all night and slept all day.

No comma is needed before *and* in this sentence because it merely divides the parts of a double predicate: the two verbs, *worked* and *slept,* are dependent on the single grammatical subject *he.* You can, if you like, use a comma in such a construction, but its use would be to indicate a pause rather than to point the structure of the sentence.

Use a Comma after Certain Sorts of Introductory Elements

> Years ago, when we were young, we would slip off to the theater downtown.
>
> Once the lights went down and the music came up, we knew that we were going to have a good time.

At the same time, we knew it was not the kind of movie that we should be seeing.

This use of commas serves both to mark the structure of the sentence, setting off dependent elements from the main statement, and to indicate the pauses of speech.

In a short sentence one can just as easily leave the comma out as put it in:

When the show was over we went home.

Use a Comma Between the Items in a Series

The recipe calls for eggs, butter, milk, and cheese.

The cook must then beat the eggs, melt the butter, heat the milk, and grate the cheese.

The result should be a rich, light, fluffy souffle.

Note | In a sentence like the last one, there is never a comma between the last adjective and the noun. In the first two examples, some editors would omit the comma before the *and;* to do so seems a doubtful economy.

Use Commas to Set Off Parenthetic Elements

This rule rests on the troublesome distinction between what are called restrictive and nonrestrictive elements. A clause, a phrase, or a word that is not essential to the meaning of a sentence is said to be nonrestrictive (or parenthetical), thus:

The recipe is, for the most part, easy to follow.

Marylou asked the chef, who was right in the middle of whisking an omelette, to come help her with the fondue.

In both of these examples, the phrases set off by commas, although important to the full sense of what is said, could be omitted without destroying the main statement. The case is different with restrictive elements. Suppose that the second example read:

Three of the chefs were not busy then, but Marylou asked the chef who was right in the middle of whisking an omelette to come help her with the fondue.

The relative clause beginning with *who* is now interpreted as essential to the sense—of the several chefs, just that one so identified is meant; the clause is therefore restrictive and is not set off by commas.

The troublesome part of the distinction between restrictive and nonrestrictive elements can be illustrated by this sentence:

Albert Einstein, who was a scientist, loved to play the violin.

One can hardly say that being a scientist is a nonessential or merely parenthetic fact about Einstein. The fact, however, is not essential to the statement that he loved to play the violin, and so the *who* clause is treated as nonrestrictive, even though it is certainly a logically necessary part of our idea of Einstein.

If you decide that an element is nonrestrictive or parenthetic and should be set off by commas, be sure to complete the job—don't use one comma where two are needed:

Not: Our waiter, the one with the little mustache and the tinted glasses looks tired.
But: Our waiter, the one with the little mustache and the tinted glasses, looks tired.

Semicolon

Separate the Main Clauses of a
Compound Sentence by a Semicolon
If There Is No Connecting Word Between Them

We waited patiently for the dessert; it never did arrive.

The bill did not take long to come; the waiter brought it quickly.

Jane slammed the restaurant door behind her; "wait till Michelin hears this," she said.

Exception | For certain effects of rapidity or close sequence— usually when the sentence is short—the comma may be substituted for the usual semicolon:

Some giggled, others laughed, a few looked grave.

Separate the Main Clauses of a Compound Sentence by a Semicolon If They Are Joined by a Conjunctive Adverb

The waiter was not to blame; indeed, he was trying his best to calm the chef.

This kind of sentence, in which the two parts are linked by a conjunctive adverb ("indeed"), is important to recognize. Like a coordinating conjunction (see p. 32), a conjunctive adverb links the halves of a compound sentence, but it marks a stronger break in thought or structure than a coordinating conjunction does and therefore requires a stronger mark of punctuation—a semicolon rather than a comma.

Since there are only seven coordinating conjunctions (listed on p. 32), if you know them you can quickly identify the conjunctive adverbs by process of elimination. The conjunctive adverbs are many—for example, these:

after all	indeed
also	in fact
besides	instead
consequently	moreover
furthermore	still
hence	therefore
however	thus

And many more. Note that most of the conjunctive adverbs are followed by a comma:

> The chef was apoplectic; indeed, he never recovered from the shock.

Note | The most common blunder in the punctuation of sentences consists in using a comma when a semicolon is needed; this is the fault called "comma splice" or simply "comma fault," as though it alone were *the* error in the use of commas. It is easy to recognize if you try:

> Frankenstein never seemed so exciting before, however, I had been expected at home for hours by now.
> (*Wrong:* replace the comma with a semicolon before the conjunctive adverb *however.*)
>
> Frankenstein had an unhappy youth, he was not accepted by his peers.
> (*Wrong:* the two independent clauses must be separated by a semicolon if they are not treated as separate sentences.)
>
> Frankenstein was in great form, and I had a whole afternoon free in which to watch him work.
> (*Quite right:* the coordinating conjunction *and* requires only the comma before it.)

Use a Semicolon to Punctuate a Series of Phrases or Word Groups Already Containing Commas

> *Frankenstein* will be shown at 10:00 A.M., Tuesday, February 4; at 11:30 A.M., Wednesday, February 5; and at 10:45 A.M., Friday, February 7.

The function of the semicolon here is solely to mark off clearly one unit from the next. If the parts of the series are clear enough through the use of commas only, then the semicolon should not be used:

> *Frankenstein* will be shown on Tuesday at 10:00 A.M., on Wednesday at 11:30 A.M., and on Friday at 10:45 A.M.

Colon

The colon is the strongest mark of internal punctuation and should be used sparingly. It marks the strong pause before a list, an example or illustration, a quotation:

> I wish to acknowledge the assistance of the following authorities: Frederick Bracher, Thomas Johnston, Marion Stocking, and Robert Waddell.

> The point was clear enough: if you want to play you'll have to join the club.

> Macaulay liked to quote Bentley's remark: "No man was ever written down but by himself."

Note | Don't use a colon to break up a close grammatical sequence such as follows forms of the verb *to be:*
> The ingredients of a good omelette are: the freshest eggs and the lightest hand.

No punctuation should be used at the point where the colon has been intruded.

Dash

The dash is used to indicate a break or sudden turn in the development of a sentence:

> What you have to do first—I think I remember the recipe—is to catch your hare.

Dashes are also used to set off explanations or definitions:

> Jugged hare—no jug is used anymore—is still a popular dish in London restaurants.

You can insert anything into a sentence if you put it between dashes, but if that method is much used the style of your sentences will grow loose to the point of dissolution. Dashes should therefore be used rather sparingly.

Apostrophe and Quotation Marks

Strictly and simply, the apostrophe is used to form the possessive:

> A man's abilities and a man's fame do not always match.

The apostrophe is also used to indicate contractions:

> I can't think why you don't agree.

In equally simple terms, quotation marks are used to mark quotations:

> According to Oscar Wilde's instructive epigram, "all art is quite useless."
>
> The last thing that she said was "don't call me; I'll call you."

The convention in the United States is to use double marks of quotation (" ") as the standard. Quotations within quotations are set off by single marks (' '):

> "Well, mother," she sighed; "I hope you're not going to say what you said last week: 'be sure to be home before midnight.'"

For further discussion of the mechanics of quotation, see *Quotations*, pp. 42–45.

Quotation marks may also identify words used not in their normal way but isolated as the subjects of discussion:

> The words "check enclosed" are the most beautiful in the English language.
>
> Mary uses "this" too often in her sentences.

For the use of quotation marks around titles, see *Titles*, p. 57.

Punctuation for Emphasis

In order to call special attention to a word or phrase one may <u>underline</u> it, or put it in "quotation marks," or put it in CAPI-TALS, or add an exclamation mark! In general, try to write so that emphasis is created by your choice of language and the structure of your sentences, not by the mechanical means of typography and punctuation: underlining and exclamation marks are poor substitutes for good sense and eloquence. If, in your judgment, only special punctuation will do the job, remember that the effect of such devices dwindles with each repetition. Be SPARING in <u>your</u> use of these "things"!

Mechanics: Spelling, Word Division, Capitalization

> "Do you spell it with a 'V' or a 'W'?" inquired the judge. "That depends upon the taste and fancy of the speller, my Lord," replied Sam.
> —Charles Dickens, *Pickwick Papers*

All of these matters are treated authoritatively in any desk dictionary. They have no clear principle other than usage, and that is not to be taught in any brief way: experience modified by good sense is the only guide.

Spelling   sp

It may be of some assistance to know that the ten words or word groups most frequently misspelled have been identified as these:

their	two	receive	exist	occur
there	too	receiving	existence	occurred
they're	to		existent	occurring
				occurrence
definite	believe	separate	occasion	lose
definitely	belief	separation		losing

Word Division

In general, break words between syllables; a desk dictionary will quickly settle any doubtful cases.

Avoid breaking proper names. In printed matter where a justified, or straight, right-hand margin is used, it is sometimes impractical to follow this rule. But in typed or handwritten work, you should always start a new line rather than write, for example,

Ernest Hem-

ingway.

cap *Capitalization*

Proper names—that is, the names of particular places and persons—are regularly capitalized:

> Chicago
> Graham Greene
> Lake Geneva

So are titles when they are connected with proper names:

> Chairman Mao
> Professor O'Brien

Questions arise when the words are special but not strictly proper names: First Great Growth Claret; a truly notable Work of Art; a World-Class tennis player. The best advice, when you are tempted to break out in capitals in that way, is Don't.

Titles of books, magazines, plays, movies, paintings, and the like are capitalized. (They may also be *italicized* or placed within quotation marks; see *Titles,* p. 56.)

A SHORT STYLE SHEET

"Style" in the phrase "style sheet" does not mean the expressive character of one's writing but rather the rules for handling the conversion of the spoken word into the conventions of written form; "editorial style" is an alternative term. Every publication, every profession and discipline, has its own variations of the rules, and they have to be learned as occasion requires. What follows is a general outline only, subject to much particular modification. The directions are for typescript, but apply to writing in longhand as well.

Format

What you write is written to be read; it should therefore be legible. To insure that it is, avoid all eccentricities and follow the standard requirements listed below. Obviously, every sort of messiness is undesirable: there is no reason why a reader should care about a paper whose writer has not cared enough to make it presentable.

41

1. Use standard-sized (8½" × 11") plain white sheets of paper—not ruled, not onionskin, not torn from a spiral notebook.

2. Double space between lines, except in block quotations (see *Longer Quotations,* p. 43).

3. Leave an adequate margin (1 to 1½ inches) on all sides of the paper: top, bottom, left, right.

4. Use one side of the paper only.

5. Identify the paper clearly:
   a. Provide a title, either on a separate title page or at the head of the first page.
   b. Put your name on the paper.
   c. Number the pages, beginning with the first page of the text.

6. Papers written in longhand must be in ink. They should also be written on wide-ruled theme paper and be double-spaced, that is, written on every other line. In all other ways they should follow the rules for the format of typed papers.

Quotations

Accuracy   Always quote accurately. Even minor mistakes in transcribing a passage damage a reader's confidence in the reliability of the writer.

Brief Quotations   Quotations of not more than four lines of prose or two lines of verse are placed between quotation marks and made a part of your own text:

> The Connecticut Yankee learns that "you can't throw too much style into a miracle. It costs trouble, and work, and sometimes money; but it pays in the end."

In quoting a brief passage of verse, you may indicate line division by a slash, and by keeping the capital letter at the beginning of the next line:

As Auden said of poetry, "it survives / In the valley of its saying."

Note that a quotation which you have made a part of your own sentence must be compatible with the grammar and punctuation of your own sentence. This may mean that you have to make some adjustments to the punctuation of the quotation or that you may have to revise the structure of your sentence.

Longer Quotations   Quotations of more than four type-written lines of prose or two lines of verse are not put within quotation marks but are indented and single-spaced: the form is called block quotation. The special typographical form indicates that you are quoting, so that no quotation marks are needed (unless, of course, they are part of what you are quoting):

> Vladimir Nabokov's defense of *Lolita* is witty but evasive:
>
>> Teachers of Literature are apt to think up such problems as "What is the guy trying to say?" Now, I happen to be the kind of author who in starting to work on a book has no other purpose than to get rid of that book and who, when asked to explain its origin and growth, has to rely on such ancient terms as Interreaction of Inspiration and Combination—which, I admit, sounds like a conjurer explaining one trick by performing another.
>
> It is not necessary to know Dr. Isaac Watts's *The Sluggard* in order to enjoy Lewis Carroll's parody of that moral poem:
>
>> 'Tis the voice of the Lobster; I heard him declare,
>> "You have baked me too brown, I must sugar my hair."
>> As a duck with its eyelids, so he with his nose
>> Trims his belt and his buttons, and turns out his toes.

Omissions   Omissions in quoted material are indicated by spaced periods called ellipses. Do not put marks of omission at the beginning or end of quotations. It is understood that such quotations are parts taken from a larger whole. When people complain of being quoted "out of context," they forget that all quotations are out of context: that is the only way anything can be quoted. Marks of omission at the beginning or end are an indication of that absent context which any reader knows is absent.

Indicate *internal* omissions by three spaced periods (. . . not ...):

> Howard Mumford Jones tells us that "Diamond Jim Brady . . . collected chorus girls, Oriental rugs, prize fighters, automobiles, bicycles, pictures—anything and everything."

If the omission occurs at the end of a sentence, use four periods, one of which indicates that a sentence has ended within the matter being quoted:

> Jones adds these details about Brady:
>> He once bought a gold-and-white piano for four thousand dollars. . . . He had a Turkish room in The Rutland, an apartment house, studded with hand-painted coal scuttles, pyrographic work, burnt-leather cushions, gilded rolling pins, and inlaid tabourets.

To indicate the omission of a line or more of verse use a line of spaced periods:

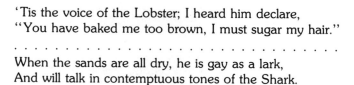

> 'Tis the voice of the Lobster; I heard him declare,
> "You have baked me too brown, I must sugar my hair."
> . . . .
> When the sands are all dry, he is gay as a lark,
> And will talk in contemptuous tones of the Shark.

Large omissions—a paragraph or more—in block quotations of prose may also be indicated by a full line of spaced periods, but it is the more usual practice to use only four spaced periods for that purpose.

Editorial Additions or Alterations   Any change that you make in a quoted passage (usually to adjust it to the structure of your own text or to add information) must be indicated with square brackets [   ]. Since they are not part of the standard typewriter keyboard, they must be put in by hand:

> "With sobs and tears [the walrus] sorted out / Those of the largest size."

Acknowledgments and Footnotes

Acknowledgments

The propriety of acknowledging indebtedness is clear, but how to do it is not always quite so clear. Matter that you quote is evidently acknowledged to belong to someone else by the fact that you treat it as a quotation. Ideas that you reexpress in your own language are the problem, since you have in some way made them your own by the act of translation. But any time that you are conscious that what you write has been borrowed from someone else, the fact should be acknowledged.

If the borrowing is general, then provide a general acknowledgment. Usually this should appear in the paper itself, not as an item tucked away in a bibliography at the end.

> The section on German wines is based on the description in Frank Schoonmaker, *The Wines of Germany,* revised edition, New York, 1974. All the figures on production and all statements about wine laws are taken from that source.

For particular passages taken from particular sources, whether paraphrased or quoted, one uses footnotes.

Footnotes

Footnotes are of two kinds: either they make a specific acknowledgment of a source, or they add some information to the material of the main text. Strictly, a footnote is a note that is placed at the foot of a page; but the term is stretched to include notes put at the end of a text.

The form of footnotes is susceptible of indefinite variation, but the elements of the form can be quickly learned in the following rules.

A. Number each footnote consecutively (the sequence can begin over again with each new page or section, or it can be maintained through the whole). Place a superscript number at the point in the text to which the note refers. No punctuation is used after this number:

> As Auden said of poetry, "it survives/In the valley of its saying." [1]

The note is then placed at the foot of the page. How much space must be reserved for the notes on any given page is difficult to estimate; it is for this reason mainly that writers prefer the system of putting all notes on a separate sheet at the end of the paper. If notes are put at the foot of the page, the usual scheme is to type an unbroken line, twenty spaces wide, between text and footnote(s); two lines below this is placed, indented, the superscript number corresponding to that in the text. The note then follows:

1
"In Memory of W. B. Yeats," lines 36-37.

B. Footnotes adding information to the main text—dates, opinions, identifications, explanations, cross-references, whatever—have no special requirements of form. They may, however, quickly become a vice. If the material is worth including, ask yourself whether it can be incorporated in your text. If it can't, do you really need it? Sometimes the answer will be yes, but not always.

C. In a footnote whose function is to identify a source, the object is to make the identification both as distinct and as economical as possible. That means, usually, giving the author, title, and page number of the book:

[1]Jacques Barzun, *Simple and Direct,* p. 103.

The form of citation just given is a minimum for a full note (except for a parenthetical note, which can be shorter—see p. 53). A date helps to make the reference more distinct and may frequently be a useful clue toward placing the character and authority of the reference among works of scholarship and theory:

[1]Jacques Barzun, *Simple and Direct* (1975), p. 103.

Place and publisher may also be added, although they are less necessary to the work of identification, especially when current books are being cited:

[1]Jacques Barzun, *Simple and Direct* (New York: Harper and Row, 1975), p. 103.

Such information can, however, be important:

[2]H. W. Fowler, *A Dictionary of Modern English Usage* (Oxford: Oxford University Press, 1926).

Here, the date, publisher, and place suggest that the treatment of the subject in Fowler's book will be very different from that in a contemporary American work like Barzun's.

Once a reference has been identified, it is convenient to cite it in short form thereafter. The abbreviations *ibid.* ("in the same place") and *op. cit.* ("the work cited") are traditional scholarly formulas for doing that, but they are yielding to the more sensible, clearer practice of naming the work in short form:

[1]Barzun, *Simple and Direct,* p. 103.

If the situation is one in which there can be no possible confusion or uncertainty:

¹Barzun, p. 103.

or:

¹*Simple and Direct,* p. 103.

When you are referring to only one book, or have a long uninterrupted stretch of references to the same book, then, of course, the brief *ibid.* is the simplest way in which to make repeated references. (See also *Parenthetical Notes,* p. 53.)

When the book you are citing is one that may be found in many editions, it is essential to specify the edition that you are using:

> ***Not:***   Mark Twain, *Huckleberry Finn,* p. 109.
> ***But:***   Mark Twain, *Huckleberry Finn* (New York: New American Library, 1959), p. 109.

Of the many hundreds of editions of *Huckleberry Finn,* probably no two have the same pagination, so that a page reference to an unidentified edition is futile. In citing long works that may be found in many editions, it is often helpful to give chapter numbers as well; that way, a reader with an edition different from yours still has an approximate guide to the place cited from a long text.

Note that many books have titles and publishing details of a greater length and complexity than is required to meet the purposes of a useful footnote. Decide what you need and select accordingly.

Note also that some works—the Bible, a standard dictionary, the plays of Shakespeare or any other recognized classic work—have such currency and such fixed form that only a passing reference is needed in order to specify the place quoted:

¹Mark 4:10.
²*Hamlet,* III. i. 56–60.
³*The Inferno,* XXIV, 16–17.

If you are quoting from these with the expectation that what you quote will be recognized, no note at all is needed, or wanted.

Footnote logic may be briefly set forth:

1. Keep your footnote style consistent.
2. Keep notes brief and distinct.
3. Don't note statements that are common knowledge or uncontroversial or otherwise lack the identity and specificity that alone justify a citation.
4. Don't use more notes than you need. Writing lots of notes may give an impressive appearance to your composition, but it may also lead you to confuse the appearance of a complicated apparatus with real substance.*

Sample Footnotes

Different academic and professional disciplines have distinctly different footnote conventions. They are, however, only variations on these common forms. For a full discussion of the subject, consult Kate Turabian, *A Manual for Writers of Term Papers, Theses, and Dissertations,* 4th ed., Chicago, University of Chicago Press, 1973.

General Forms   These are suitable for any writing addressed to a general, unspecialized public, including most writing in the humanities and liberal arts.

a. A book by a single author:

[1]James Beard, *Beard on Bread* (1974), p. 30.

or:

[1]James Beard, *Beard on Bread* (New York: Alfred A. Knopf, 1974), p. 30.

b. A book compiled by an editor:

[2]Craig Claiborne, ed., *The New York Times Cook Book* (1961), p. 30.

* Suppose, when you look down, all you find is something pointless, like this?

c. An edited reprint:

> [3]P. Morton Shand, *A Book of French Wines,* ed. Cyril Ray (Penguin Books, 1964), p. 30.

d. A book with two or three authors:

> [4]M. A. Amerine and M. A. Joslyn, *Table Wines: The Technology of Their Production in California* (Berkeley, 1951), p. 30.

e. A book with more than three authors:

> [5]Wonona W. Chang et al., *An Encyclopedia of Chinese Food and Cooking* (New York, 1970), p. 30.

f. A book with a corporate or institutional author:

> [6]The Australian Wine Board, *Wine—Australia: A Guide to Australian Wine* (Melbourne, 1968), p. 30.

g. Articles in periodicals:

> [7]Jim Hicks, "Yellow Rosé of Texas," *American Wine Society Journal,* 7 (1975), 37–39.

Note that this simple form depends on the journal's being organized into volumes with continuous pagination. Many are not; in that case, a precise specification of the date will do the job, as in the examples that follow. Note too that the abbreviations *p.* or *pp.* are used before the page number(s) if no volume number is given.

MONTHLY:

> [8]Joseph Wechsberg, "Paris Journal," *Gourmet,* April 1976, pp. 10–12; 59–60.

WEEKLY:

> [9]"The California Wine Rush," *Time,* 1 March 1971, p. 76.

DAILY NEWSPAPER:

[10]Nathan Chroman, "Los Angeles County Fair Wine Judging," *Los Angeles Times,* 14 October 1975, Part VI, p. 36.

For a full treatment of the conventions of scholarly style in the humanities, especially in the matter of footnotes, consult the *MLA Style Sheet,* 2nd ed., 1970.

Forms for Scientific Writing   The reference style in both the natural and social sciences generally differs from that in other kinds of academic writing. The standard method is to avoid footnotes by listing all references in alphabetical sequence at the end of the paper; two or more works by the same author are arranged chronologically:

> Amerine, M. A. 1953. New controlled fermentation equipment at Davis. Wines and Vines *34,* No. 9, 27–30.
>
> Amerine, M. A. 1958. Aldehyde formation in submerged cultures of *Saccharomyces beticus.* Appl. Microbiol. *6,* 160–168.
>
> Amerine, M. A., Roessler, E. B., and Filipello, F. 1959. Sensory evaluation of wine. Hilgardia *28,* 477–567.
>
> Anon. 1950. Jerez, Xeres, sherry. Bull. Office Intern. Vin. *23,* No. 233, 22–33.

All citations of authorities are made, not by footnotes, but by short parenthetical references in the text itself to the authorities listed at the end:

> Amerine (1953) describes the press in critical detail.
>
> The intensity should be determined by a standard colorimeter (Amerine et al. 1959).

An alternate method identifies authorities by numbers in a single sequence:

> The method is based on reports made by committees of the National Safety Council (1) and the American Medical Association (2).

The works thus cited (and several works may be grouped together under one number when feasible) are then arranged in a single list at the end:

1. Committee on Tests for Intoxication. Report . . . to Street and Highway Section. Chicago; National Safety Council; 1938.
2. Committee to Study Problems of Motor Vehicle Accidents, American Medical Association. (Organization Section. Reports of Officer.) J. Amer. Med. Ass. *124:* 1290–1292, 1944.

A third method combines the two already described. References are arranged alphabetically at the end and are numbered:

1. Amerine, M. A. 1953. New controlled fermentation equipment at Davis. Wines and Vines *34,* No. 9, 27–30.
2. Amerine, M. A. 1958. Aldehyde formation in submerged cultures of *Saccharomyces beticus.* Appl. Microbiol. *6,* 160–168.

References in the text are then made by number rather than by name or date:

Amerine (1) describes the press in critical detail.

The intensity should be determined by a standard colorimeter (2).

Note that, in the interests of economy, all scientific references abbreviate the titles of journals:

J. Am. Chem. Soc.

Bull. Amer. Math. Soc.

In the second instance above, note too that italics are not used. Many scientific references also eliminate all but the first capital in citing books:

N. V. Sidgwick, *The electronic theory of valency,* Clarendon Press, Oxford, 1927.

They may also dispense with italics as well:

A. J. Winkler, General viticulture, University of California, Berkeley, 1962.

For authoritative guidance to the styles preferred by the various sciences consult these standard references:

biology   Council of Biology Editors, Committee on Form and Style, *CBE Style Manual,* 3rd ed., Washington, D.C., American Institute of Biological Sciences, 1972.

chemistry   "Notice to Authors of Papers" in first number of each annual volume of *Journal of the American Chemical Society.*

mathematics   American Mathematical Society, "Manual for Authors of Mathematical Papers," Providence, R.I., American Mathematical Society, 1962.

physics   American Institute of Physics, *Style Manual for Guidance in the Preparation of Papers,* rev. ed., New York, American Institute of Physics, 1973.

psychology   American Psychological Association, *Publication Manual,* 2nd ed., Washington, D.C., American Psychological Association, 1974.

Parenthetical Notes

Even in nonscientific writing, both readers and writers find short and unobtrusive parenthetical notes a convenient substitute for the more elaborate device of numbered footnotes. The parenthetical note is a brief identification that goes into the text itself immediately following the passage to be noted or at the end of a sentence if the passage is integrated into your own sentence. It may also be used after a block quotation. The parenthetical note is usually dependent on a previous footnote in which the source has been fully identified, permitting the short parenthetical form to be used thereafter. You may use the footnote to explain what your practice will be:

> [1]Leon D. Adams, *The Wines of America* (Boston: Houghton Mifflin, 1973), pp. x–xi. Subsequent references to this book will appear in the text.

The subsequent references in the text will look like this:

> (Adams, *Wines of America*, p. 10)

If, as is very likely, there is no chance of confusing the reference with anything similar, shorten it even more:

> (*Wines of America*, p. 10)

or:

> (Adams, p. 10)

or simply:

> (p. 10)

Good sense and circumstance should usually tell you what is best to do in these matters.

Note that if the passage quoted before a parenthetical note has no special punctuation then it is simply closed by quotation marks before the parenthesis. The period follows the note:

> Hank Morgan is depressed by the stale jokes of King Arthur's court: "the only right way," he says, "to classify the majestic ages of some of those jokes was by geologic periods" (*Connecticut Yankee*, p. 33).

If the passage ends with a question mark or an exclamation point, that punctuation is retained inside the quotation marks:

> Morgan worries about the artistic insufficiency of the Arthurian style: "what would this barren vocabulary get out of the mightiest spectacle—the burning of Rome in Nero's time, for instance?" (*Connecticut Yankee*, p. 94).

Bibliography

"Bibliography" is a word meaning a number of different things, some highly technical and some quite vaguely general. Most often, it is used to name a list of books and references that might better be called "A List of Works Consulted" or "A List of Works Cited." Most short papers really have no need for such a list, if the work of citation has been honestly and distinctly done in the course of the paper itself (scientific papers are an exception: see *Forms for Scientific Writing*, p. 51). But such lists may be very useful at the end of longer papers in which many different authorities have been repeatedly used. The entries are arranged alphabetically by author, the names are inverted, the punctuation is rather heavy, and the transcription of title, place, publisher, and date is fuller than in an ordinary note. Note too that it is not the first line but the second and following lines that are indented.

Sample bibliography entries:

Beard, James. *Beard on Bread.* New York: Alfred A. Knopf, 1973.

Rombauer, Irma S., and Marion Rombauer Becker. *Joy of Cooking.* Indianapolis: Bobbs-Merrill, [1964].

Note that only the first of the two authors' names is inverted; note also the bracketed date, indicating that the book carries no date on its title page and that the information has been supplied from some other source, usually the copyright page.

Shand, P. Morton. *A Book of French Wines.* Revised and edited by Cyril Ray. Harmondsworth: Penguin Books, 1964 (contrast the sample footnote entry for this same title on p. 50).

Bell, Kenneth. "English Cheese." *Wine and Food,* No. 131 (Autumn 1966), pp. 34–38.

Miscellaneous Conventions

The Use of *Italics,* or <u>Underlining</u>

Italic type, represented by underlining in typewritten and handwritten texts, is a way of indicating a number of special situations, among them:

A.   Foreign words and phrases, if they are still recognized as foreign, are italicized. One would italicize *modus vivendi* or *comme il faut.* But if the word or phrase is familiarly used in English, leave it alone: a la mode, a priori, Realpolitik, mañana, maestro, and the like would never be italicized. Some terms are borderline cases: savoir faire, quid pro quo, or Bildungsroman, for example, might or might not be italicized, according to the taste of the writer, the context, and the character of the audience. If you are undecided about a particular word, you might check your dictionary. Some dictionaries do indicate whether words are generally italicized or not.

B.   Words treated as words may be put either in quotation marks (see *Apostrophe and Quotation Marks,* p. 38) or in italics.

C.   Italics also indicate emphasis: see *Punctuation for Emphasis,* p. 39.

D.   Titles of certain kinds of works are italicized: see the next section for a discussion of this matter.

Titles

A.   The first word and the main terms in titles are capitalized:

> *Gone with the Wind*
> *Far from the Madding Crowd*
> "The Short Happy Life of Francis Macomber"
> *The Journal of the American Society of Enologists*

B. The titles of books, magazines, newspapers, plays, long poems, and movies should be italicized. So should the names of ships:

> When he crossed on the *Queen Elizabeth II* he read *Captains Courageous.*

C. The titles of short stories, short poems, articles, essays, chapters, and songs are not italicized but are put within quotation marks. Generally, the choice between italics or quotation marks is determined by the length of the work.

> The poem that the narrator quotes in Thurber's "The Waters of the Moon" is Browning's "Caliban."
>
> "My Favorite Things" was the hit song in *The Sound of Music.*

Numbers

Spell out numbers of one or two digits; use numerals for the rest:

> One of the four beasts gave unto the seven angels seven golden vials.
>
> The mark of the Beast is 666.

Do not spell out numbers in dates or page references:

> December 25 is mentioned on page 2.

If you are using numbers frequently or writing a statistical paper, then the rule about spelling out numbers no longer applies: use numerals instead. But never *begin* any sentence with numerals, no matter what sort of paper you may be writing.

Abbreviations

Academic writing has accumulated a number of abbreviated Latin terms—e.g., i.e., ibid., cf., q.v., op. cit., and the like—whose proper place is in footnotes, where they save space, rather than in the text, where they are a kind of hiccups. When you use them, do not italicize them. Above all, be sure that you know what they mean (they may be found in any dictionary): i.e. does not mean what e.g. does, nor q.v. what cf. does. Note that i.e., e.g., ibid., q.v., op. cit. are set off by commas; but cf. (meaning "compare") is not.

The familiar abbreviation "etc." should be avoided except in notes. It very often signifies merely that the writer is gesturing toward what he means rather than denoting it clearly. "And etc." is doubly objectionable, since the phrase "et cetera" already contains the Latin word for "and." If your enumeration does not need to be complete, use a phrase such as "and so on" or "and the like."

Acronyms, words made from the initial letters of a name or title (GASP = Group Against Smog Pollution), are a standard part of the American language now—we live in a world of NOW, CORE, SWAT, WAR, CARE, SNAKE, and other striking creations, not to mention the myriad federal and state agencies whose names are strings of unexpressive initials —NLRB, FETC, BATF. Many acronyms and initialisms— UNESCO, GOP—are immediately recognizable and need no explanation. For others, it may be necessary at first use to spell out what the letters stand for; once that is done, use the short form, which is less an abbreviation than a name. It requires no period after the letters, as an abbreviation would.

Other abbreviations, as a rule, are to be avoided, unless they are appropriate to the tone of what you are writing. Using S.P. instead of Southern Pacific is like using a nickname—appropriate to designedly informal writing but not otherwise.